Praise for
Imponderables Propel the Dance: The Russian Collection

These poems of Alex Levitch's are a unique dive, not only into the marrow of the man himself, a man who, like all good pirates, has plundered the world both externally and internally, but also into Russia's mysterious Faberge egg.

Alex was there - as a pirate, as a man, as a son and grandson. These poems will take you to a young woman adjusting her makeup in a tank's rear view mirror... as that tank is shelling the Russian Parliament. Many other dreams await you. Thank you, Alex Levitch, for letting us glimpse this hidden world - the world of Mother Russia, and, of course, the world of you.

> - **David Field**, screenwriter, producer - *Amazing Grace and Chuck*, and poet - *Root Chakra Plus One*

Alex's poetry delights as do Lermontov, Pushkin, Hardy, and Frost. It invites the reader into the world of the poet – an exquisite kaleidoscope of images, textures, and sensations - all deeply felt and artfully captured.

> - **David Deaver Brown** - Simply Media, publisher of audio books

These poems are serious, clever, heart-felt, musical, focused, and original. It's a joy to take the voyage Mr. Levitch takes us on. Like its perfect, rich, evocative and mysterious title, the poems suggest, paint, evoke and lead us into the corners of the mysterious and the life and mind of the poet.

> - **Jane Marla Robbins**, author *Poems of The Laughing Buddha* and *Dogs In Topanga*.

Imponderables

Propel the Dance:

The Russian Collection

Alex Levitch

Library of Congress Control Number: 2019918889

ISBN: 978-0-578-60048-2

Printed and bound in Canada by Art Bookbindery

TABLE OF CONTENTS

Despair

Oblivion

Wonder

Fate

TRYPTIC IN 3D

A Night in Calcutta

In the dim, sulfuric pale,

    Blind sadhu finds his eyes.
        Lord Vishnu's most fantastic
        Sound and light is poised to
Begin its nightly run.

Street people pull up lawn chairs --
Argue over TV soap operas.

They make for tiny figurines:
Seekers, chatterers,
    Barbers, urchins,
        Bridesmaids, tailors,
Butchers, street-wives,
    Temple priests,
           And sari weavers.

Human figurines,
Like so many colored pool balls
   Ricocheting off each other
   On the break,
Fierce, kinetic energy.
   To the point where, finally,
Newton's laws begin to have effect.

So many streamers
Woven into one coat of many colors.
Until in the eye of Kali's breath,
Passing fire mouth-to-mouth --

Devil take the straggler –
In frenetic hunger for the feast...
Finally, freezing like a cryogenic,

Slowly into
Pre-ordained
Master sketch position
To prepare the evening toilet
And to relieve eternal boredom
-- Where, one by one,
A random few
     Drop through....

Moscow Nights

A sleek black Mercedes
pulls up to the curb.
A man in patent alligator shoes
steps out from behind
the tinted glass.
Men in black rush to his either side.
A brightly painted girl
offers up her bouquet.
The man in alligator shoes
weighs his options,
nods his head.
Flowers are purchased,
the girl is taken.

*

An old soldier passes by.
Ancient medals pinned
to threadbare suit
weight down his heart.
He lowers his head
as if in shame
for surviving so long
in enemy territory.

*

A mother with tattered child
stands quietly lost, nearby.
The old soldier
takes out a crumpled ruble note from
a beaten-up, outside pocket,
stuffs it into outreached palm
and shuffles hurriedly away.

In a miniature church
around the corner
black clad priests
slap at their collective girth,
synchronize their Rolexes,
begin their patent incantations.
Wax flames dance on
favored imitation icons.

                    *

And, so, a miniscule human mass
sways and genuflects
to a deep, melodic chorus,
exorcizing
its latest demons.

                    *

In a separate world --
its oil slicks fenced off
from nearby bathers
scrubbing off their toil.

The city of reductionists
breathes a sigh:

The Motherland is secured –
For another night!

The just man
is covered up in shadow.

A Night in Atlantic City

The hermaphrodite at the counter
waves hello.
'Come on in, dearie
you can't go wrong.'

-- A street fair barker
loaded up with Kewpie dolls,
sets up the green-glass coke bottles
essential for the game.

For any drunk
fool enough
to enter heaven, why
when there is only hell?

A pause and a jolt,
static on the line,
strobes in my head --
'Can this be all bad?'

'Timothy Leary,
where have you gone?
When were you last seen?
What have you been?'

Red lipstick
spits from the she-man's mouth.
'Come on in, 'hon--
keep your pecker on.'

I am rolling
rolling, down a slope.
The sign says,
'no freaks allowed.'

She is knocking.
I am knocking.
Someone is knocking
on my head.

The king flea
pulls the chariot.
The child flea
pushes the pin.

The boy waves hello,
'Come on in.
See the last, great ci-i-i-rcus
mag-ni-fied.'

You pays your pennies;
you gets your wishes.
Be real careful --
lest they come true.

The hermaphrodite
holds out the ticket.
Thin, veined fingers
pick dust from air.

'Come over here,
We won't bite,'
mouth, spewed with spittle,
speaks from a vacuum.

I am spinning
like a gravity ball,
suspended between beams,
e-lec-tro-static-ly.

Air is thinner here.
Jaws work like fish
whose gills won't function,
mouthing, wordlessly:

'Ta-ra-ta--taa---taa....
tit-te-ra--ta----taa....'
Faces lose their voices,
silence hangs its laundry.

Mutes and carnies,
(Greeks called them 'stoics'),
unnatural mannequins,
stare back vacuous and still.

Marionettes in wax,
their straitjackets worn
in lockstep fashion,
close ranks around my soul.

Tiny flames begin
to lick my bowels
as fire ants carry on
their mi-cro-cosm.

I descend
(or, is it 'ascend'?)
the rope
-- dis-in-ter-est-ed,
should rocks be placed or not
upon the alabaster
perimeter of my tomb.

LOS ANGELES MAN

I once traveled through the marble canyons
of Santa Monica Boulevard
searching for the home of
the king of swat, queen of hop and
master of all cell phones.

I found him under the sign of *Surfer Dude*.
He lived alone in a crowd amongst his objects
atop the palisades in the eye of the Ferris wheel
behind glass walls, bullet proofed
to miracles and snow drifts of any kind.

He was fond to say,
"*hey, the game's the thing,*"
as he bet his chips, first left then right,
now black, still red –
any variation on the theme would do.
That is, until the next.

"*Taste that piece of ass, you'll never go back!*"

I found him cloaked in Kodachrome.
It shielded his screwed-up eyes
from crimes of solitude and ambivalence,
gave his skin an olive tone
made him seem invincible.

Harmonica Man

Satan measures Voluptuousness for her evening gown;
Priest confessor assays Absolution
for the begging cup.
The husband lies with Fantasy
while his cuckolded wife
salves her wounds in nickel bags
of Convolution.

The harmonica man plays a mean bar or two;
I cannot see your face.
I cannot feel your touch.

I shake my head in answer to your prayers
and slip my feet to harmonica man's beat

The harmonica man plays a mean bar or two;
half-naked women hang around his arms
and whisper huskily
of 'first takes' or 'last rites' or some such thing.
I know I am not in this picture;
it hangs in recesses
too deep for curved spaces.
But the barkeep slides another,
down the long oak pitch.
Fumes parch the throat before liquor touches lips.

I shake my head in answer to your prayers
and slip my feet to harmonica man's beat

A hundred sighs and pants accompany
hands which play a riff
along time's slender neck.
Soldiers march in single file,
listening all the while,
dressed in warm greatcoats in knee deep, centuries' old snow –

chaffing hands, telling dirty jokes, to pass their sentence
in muted tones of palmsmanship --
calm conspiracy amongst those on death row.
The air I suck chills, clogs the lungs.

I shake my head in answer to your prayers
and slip my feet to harmonica man's beat

     *

In a distant place, tunes collide in one big bang
and begin all over.
Harmonica man plays a mean bar or two;
the living dead swing their partners to doe-see-doe.
Sages wander through vacant clouds,
scratch their navels, nod their heads, stretch their beards --
protesting there must be more.

'Listen, can't you hear the saxophone
pleading -- muffled drums and castanets
moving -- you along -- to a different place?'

I shake my head in answer to your prayers
and slip my feet to harmonica man's beat

INSIDE THE MOUNTAIN: RETURN TO NOWHERE

Whispers streak through cool mountain streams
like steel locomotives bulleting straight on
impermeable, glistening, hand-spiked tracks.

Soft ground opens to reveal
a swelling of desire: summer moss,
autumn vines clinging --
halogen reflections – diffused.

The second hand holds no hostages
in this place where mountains fall aside
through clouds of frozen breath.

No soul seeks comfort here.
Wise men seek no absolutes in search of nothing.
Gods deal in relativity --

Balancing, calibrating, fornicating
on stainless scales
that go 'round and around.

ODE TO HEGEL: SIBERIA

She floats, in nightshift,
past the long, hatless, shoeless line of geks[1]
-- half-life, starving faces,
stickmen to her voluptuousness.

She is like a fat chameleon
viewing, from the redoubt of
un-touch-a-bil-ity,
moving pictures of John Cameron's
      black & white parade – passing.

She calls out in weak falsetto,
dissolving the line into a band --
smacking lips to tinsel horns,
beating bones on out-stretched skins --
      cooing to Moses, still hidden in the reeds.

She can't be seen -- only her shift,
like a comet's tail, spitting sparks,
against which slave souls bang their heads
for the ultimate dissolution --
      retrieving sunbursts in desert air.

---

[1] Prisoners of Stalin's Gulag

She'll never be unveiled!
For she's only guise, posing,
patched up from long lists of shrapnel wishes --
gekdom's dry-eyed mistress,
        teasing fool's milk out of milkless teats.

THE REEL

A lone egret
flew over from wetland
to where the thick fir stands.
There, she stirred the heart
of a forest troll.
Together, they danced the reel
and found their common god.

*

The fiddler taps his feet
and plays a reel.
Two lovers dance
to the music
-- like insomniacs.

He, all dark, boots on end,
waistcoat aflutter.
An old oak,
he holds her, in suspense,
in thick, gnarled hands --
to never let her go.

She, pale white,
with long, slender limbs,
Viking hair, arched and
translucent
in a simple shift
(or is it her wedding dress?),
glides barefoot in his strength.

The fiddler taps his feet
and plays a reel.
The two lovers depart
the world they know.

The tune defines their moment,
Its music flowing through them
like blood.

They breathe it, too.
An intoxicating ether --
it pricks their skin,
soaks into their bones.

Their universe is vast.
Their movements are eternal
and complete,
like two toy dancers
going 'round and 'round
in a child's wind-her-up
snow-capped crystal ball.

*

Meanwhile --
a one-armed madman milks his cow
while a mother marsh bird
lures the hunting dog.

A midwife cuts the cord
as Calcutta beggars
prepare their morning toilet.
Prison doors open for the rapist;
the glittering audience
swoons to Lucia's romance.
Faithful servant steals the dowry.
Teresa tends the lepers.
The hopeful soul awaits a sign
at the appointed time --
between indiscretions
and forgetfulness.

       *

Two lovers dance the reel
while a fiddler taps his feet...
and they escape it all.

TRIBUTE

I. Dusk

A letter, creased and smudged,
a hand-spun shawl she wore.

Would I have clutched only these,
        if I had seen?

But -- like Alexander,
I marched straight through the heart,
to come out the other side
        carrying but thin trophies.

And we race on -- sunbeams blinding,
glory moments kept --
like tracer flares, they swallow
the sky, through which
we are surrendered
        to mythology.

II. Dawn

A child's silvered walking shoes,
a pebble from the shores.

Faint greetings, partings,
scratched at least this once,
wishes trapped in a bottle --
tiny wing beats dissolved away,
spirits mortared
into musty wormholes --
they leave us muted
like cat tracks in snow.

A portrait from the picnic,
paper poems to secret loves.

Bits of phosphor --
tiny, slender moments, earth-bound
flotsam scattered in the wake.

Strangers reap the salvage,
before it is gone,
misplaced,
forgotten.

When Once We Were Children

Part I

Brightly colored
playing marbles,
so many peafowl
at the petting zoo,
gold specks
on morning's dew,
infinitesimal bubbles,
frozen many
millions of years ago,
in soft amber glow,
hot milk from
Mama's teat
splashed white
upon my lips,
flutter wings of
the golden moth,
dancing around
its tiny star,
the super-hero
boots I wore,
when I flew to save
Felicia,
the eagle's call
to justice
in Chapter Nine

of Everybody's
Golden Rhyme,
your hand on mine
as we climbed
the steepest cliff
to diamond valley --
your perfect smile
and tight embrace,
our secret sign
when we looked into
the other's eyes,
and saw...
ourselves --
just the two of us.

Part II

I weep
For the loss
Of my closest friends.

The troll
That governs this bridge
Has taken them.

I weep
For the loss
Of Dumpha and Bonmama

The troll
That governs this bridge
Has shot them.
I place
My hands and feet
In ice-blocks, now.

No stopping,
No staring,
No wondering, please.

It is written
What to believe,
Whom not to trust.

When no one
Is looking
Sometimes,

I am like
The starving cat
Hearing a sudden noise.

But the pain
Makes me sad,
Again.

I go to sleep,
Afraid
To wake, again.

Maybe,
they will bury me
in Diamond Valley.

Part III

Multiple gods,
a zillion odds.
Choices made

escape
retribution, but
present, instead,
everyday
opportunities for
redemption.

Innocence
is not chosen,
survival is.
Dreamtime
sublimates
playtime.

Recalled wonder
eclipses fear,
suppresses time,
steals.

Hunger rules by
Beauty's side.

Golden moments
are like these
lost trinkets,
buried in cereal boxes.

Faith

History I

A man holds in his hands
the head of his enemy
-- like Salome caressing her lover
      Dead eyes looking out, merge dully
      into his own.

Water flows through any sieve.
Tears co-mingle -- they blur the deed,
cutting deep furrows (but not deep enough)
      Into the iron mask he wears
      over his heart.

Grave markers heaped stone against stone.
A ghetto yard piles up fates
like so many playing cards.

And the Queen of spades slips
quietly by.[1]

A sea of ghosts
echoes the silent rush to self-destruction.
A barren kingdom is further
exaggerated

---

[1] From a Pushkin short story about an ancient countess who sells her soul to the Devil to win at cards (specifically, the secret of the three cards). A young, impassioned officer seduces a young caretaker and steals the old lady's secret. He wins at cards twice but loses on the third try, and then kills himself.

Our history -- madmen and hubris
set the cycles.

The last of his species, he fought
to claim relevancy
-- obliterating the descriptive, "humanity"
from the English language
  His history -- a momentary menopause
  before the emptiness.

In the belly, we know our struggle
is to deny.
Affirmation closed her shutters long ago,
when her garden withered and
the gods began to play the odds.

History II

Faith, Rationality, Probability --
the holiest of trinities -- meet
to dine on Self's daily course.
Jesus orders toast. Descartes
weighs the loaf. Bohr draws
a card. As the meal's devoured,
everything else melds into The Feast.
Now, *that* is singularity!

* * *

Joan, at the torch; Caravaggio
beatifying his Sabines; Camp doctors, the
good clerks, recording Jewish anatomy;
Smoking Joe, fighting out his heart; John Galt
at the breach, retreating to his mount;
Nero crucifying his Christians; Mahatma,
fasting, weaving cloth; Alexander,
conquering, vanquishing, surrendering;
Dante, dreaming his descent;
Arthur, his Guinevere. Socrates,

vial in hand; Onegin, at the end.

Diamond Lil met her mark, by chance,
and fell into it. Shit

happens everywhere – it is what you

make of it. Acid rain creates
multi-prism sunsets, transparent lakes.

The Taj levitates, bridal white, on the backs

of muddy slave-souls, ten thousand strong --
its black twin, Dream, buried in the dead heart
of a madman, its bastard twin, Hubris,
carried in the belly of *history's* most
pregnant masterworks.

* * *

The lioness stalks her prey,
downwind, with an appraising eye.
A giant, golden eagle surveils
the scene from on high.
Hidden in the tall grass, the emu
senses finality and begins its run --
three days meat on the hoof.
The end comes in a flash --
sinew, blood and anguish
soak into the earth,
and, then, it is forgotten.
A solitary comet arcs the
sky, tracing light back
yesteryears through its
gaseous spew.
A trillion stars
wink back in recognition,
over the span of Time & Space
and gratitude --
that we might yet
uncover the wonder within.
Jesus, Descartes and Bohr
shall dine again.

The Theory of Everything
   awaits another day unrealized
      but not yet discarded,
         as mankind struggles
            with its observation
               that we reign higher than
                  the eagle and the lion,
                     but lower than the stars.

Prayer

An old hag, slope-shouldered,
stooped and bent, invisible,
       stops to pray.

.... When misery, woe, hunger
and despondency
       shall be
          (your humble servant prays)
           transmogrified.

All God's chill'un
gots to have shoes and chitlins.
       The meek shall transmogrify.

Faithful servant to the crust,
fate roots her to the spot --
       an ancient baobab,

Marooned and bowed
to the prevailing winds,
       sponging teardrops from the plains.

Naked limbs hold her offering:
empty vessel for a kingdom,
       ashes for fire.

Blinded eyes smile surrendering,
lost loves swallowing up the residue --
Recycled hates, muttering hermits,

dreamy artists, young girls with dogs,
      men at war, entire movie casts
      tumble by --

Beyond blood, bone, roots of tears,
omnipresent plains,
      flame licks its glow.

'Vision of Mary Magdalene
or ghost reincarnate?'
      faith wants to say.
'Keeper of the desert rose
or splash of heather on lava steppes?'
      Emerson echoes back.

The gods wrap whirlwinds
      around her feet!

THIEVES

Behooded monks
dance an incantation
'round their latest illumination.
'Lord, give us leave,
so we may steal a single glance
of this, your creation.'

*

Stout legs kick up
from beneath moth-worn robes,
made crimson brown in winter's sun.
A moment's warmth steals
through priestly bones,
married to denial.

A croupier lost in time
wakes to find his cards
stuffed into the third folio
of a martyr's life.
Surreptitiously,
he steals the whole
and slinks into the void.

A child is born
and stolen that same night,
left on the stoop
of these same monks --
Original intent re-minted
to a token of 'salvation'?

A lifetime is taken
from the child in search of
perfect light.
Until he blinds
and falls dead
one crystal night.

Two millenniums later,
the croupier returns the book --
winnings enclosed.
Behooded monks encircle
the celebratory
and begin to prepare
the human sacrifice.

Love

APPARITION

She comes upon him,
mercury in a glass.
His chest heaves,
like an iron-monger's bellows.
The minute hand stills.
The second hand begins to spin.
His heart fibrillates
like a tightrope walker's balance beam.

She, an apparition
floating on refracted rays.
A penny hologram
bought from the man
who sells cheap parlor tricks.

She moves upon him,
white light from
the interrogator's lamp.
Nuclear fusion
at its sunspot best.
A floating kaleidoscope
turned inside out,
so as not to blind Jason.

He looks upon her
through cataract eyes.
A lover's prophylactic
against attic worn,
faded white,

salt flat lines
engrained in her visage.

He sees only
the red hibiscus in her hair.

Deeper Shadows

Her eyes speak of shadows:
ice shadows
somewhere in the heart --
darkened, suppressed images
like old black & whites
put to flame,
curling back upon themselves,
churning black
before open eyes
-- forever lost
in no time at all.

A few surviving embers
cling like spiders
somewhere:
faint, thin, starving
silhouettes,
in frozen wait
for the lightning bolts
and knights in shining armor --
for the girls in garlands
and chomping
white stallions --
faint, thin, starving
silhouettes,
placed on the center piece
for gods who will not come.

If I were a god
(or even a *man),*
I would take a crimson moon
and sail it like a discus
across this night.

I would hold her by the hand
and cast reflections
to stall the shadows,
and let loose the hidden light.

Hearts & Oracles

You brush my heart
with feathers from the priest.
Silver hawks circle
the occasion,
like oracles proclaiming
omens.

I hold you deep inside
where pure lungs
pump mountain air
into a secret chamber
made of golden amber
and ice blue lapis.

Who counts anymore,
my love?

There are no moments
without you --
only a blank canvas
upon which
to start over again.
Only the void:
no time, no heartbeat
no reality.

'You are my sunshine
my only sunshine;
You make me happy
when skies are grey...[1]

Tell me darling,
what caused us
to forget
the love that we have
for each other
shall all encompass
the objects of our desire?

---

[1] Country blues song recorded by Jimmie Davis and Charles Mitchell, 1939

I Open

I move among the willows
dew-wet with a glint from first light.
I sway with your soft rhythm
stirred, by still breeze of the
serpent's undulation.

Gone are thoughts of glory days
as are bitter recantations.
Gone are hot swells on crusts of dry earth;
absorbed, they recess in the
innermost folds of nowhere.

Nothing interferes, my love;
nothing chances to link the senses.
Blood pours out; ether seeps in.
I open and am vassal to the stars.

SAPPHIRES AT RIVER'S EDGE

Stay, my love.
Do you remember –

how this river winds
and meanders faithlessly
through soft, clover fields,
past shuttered citadels filled
with circumstance,
along iron tracks where
hand forged narrow gauge
marked steep descents;
how this river twists
in cyclone loops
(like the great Houdini
escaping the jacket),
never pausing in its
flowing, healing, deceiving,
calm, caressing waters
not for those innocent eyes,
not for heavenly prayer,
not even for a dying wish!

Stay my love.

We traversed this divide,
embraced only in our hearts.

51

We gorged ourselves in waters
deeper than our sorrow
more soothing than our rage
and reached within the hot
of molten fire
to pluck out
her most elusive prize:
sapphire eyes --
cool, piercing, penetrating sapphire eyes –
sparkling pathways to
transparent nakedness.

Flashing signposts --
'this way to heaven'.

Like sun-drenched neophytes,
we gulped down the water
filtered by these stones.
Don't you remember?

Tonight My Love

Cigarette smoke curling
into the air --
my thoughts spiral
along its trail.

Long, soft hair
spread fan-like on the pillow.
Beads of perspiration,
intimate whispers,
between the two of us.

I swallow long and hard
every aspect of you
and dissolve into
a million tiny stars.

THE GIRL WITH THE SEAWEED EYES

I loved her first when ice blue glaciers came,
when giant birds of paradise eclipsed the sun.
We met at the canyon's edge,
sharing our innermost secrets.
Her eyes locked mine;
sunspots danced around the core.

They were the color of seaweed --
I drowned in them.
I knew her vulnerability.
She accepted my surrender.
We rode bareback on an
enchanted pale white.

The beast's giant nostrils
flared like bellows --
forging pure oxygen into steel fire.

The white of its eyes
betrayed a delicious panic,
as we bridged chasms through its stride.

We rode furiously at first,
as if time could disappear
and there was all
to absorb of each other.
There was no need for the whip.

We had only to keep our breath,

so as not to release
our hold upon the other --
as the rabbi would hang on tightly
to his great book,
or the sculptor his last stone.

There was no need for futile hopes.
We had only to place our hearts
upon evening's table
and let the blood flow
into captive rivulets
into one liquid pool
of existential being.
(Our love had this grace
of simplicity.
No conditions, no limits,
timeless continuity.)

*

Upon a while, the steed slowed to canter.
Bright, purple cotton spores filled the air.
A fragrance of remembrance --
full moon as reflected in mist.
Images began to blur --
like penny store photogravures.

The pale white became a vague figment.
The seaweed eyes, though, never left mine.
I smothered her in orchids and sent the beast away.

TRANSPARENT

My love
I have these *desires*
to know each other's every inner fear,
to share each other's every outward tear,
to whisper wordlessly
in a language of our own,
to move as one,
languidly, through the swirl,
to hold your laughter
on the cusp with mine,
to breathe forever-in
each other's scent,
to swallow whole
this passion --
urgently, as our own,
to grasp, above all,
our supple natures,
and make transparent
our lives together.

*

My darling...
I kiss your eyes.

Hope

Anthem

Flags in multicolor flutter like impatient storks
vacillating in the wind.

Onlookers crook their heads
stirring black ink circles in the soft crust beneath
-- secret sects of Nechaevists and Banshees
-- zealots at the crossroads,
caught red-handed (stuffing hoarded jewels in mouths),
squeezing passed-on lies through thickened arteries.

They come to hail a Caesar,
force-marching two Belgian grays stolen from a Breughel
-- Scolding father to bastard sons in unquiet times

-- Savior for this night,
Immortalized in Vladimir Ilyich's darkened rendering,
hauling the Last Idea towards her funeral pyre.

*

They will say, 'She died to save us from our sins!'

They will say, 'It's time now to crush out her embers,
to celebrate the Order.'

What of the truth?' you say. *'What of beauty?'* you plead.
'What of solitude?' you cry. *'What of free...dom?'*
You whistle through your teeth.

What of it?
We suppose you will ask next about 'me' or 'you' or 'I'?
or about 'forgiveness' or of 'remembrance'?

'Well, forget it all!', a lonely soul --
made mad by the edict nature
of the conversation --
sings a refrain
in perfect acapella pitch.

'Forget it all, forget it all, forget it all

-- tralalalala… tralalalala… Harte Scheiste!'

The Living hold their breath. The Idea has died.
A steel hand of Emptiness descends.

*

In the desert surrounding,
the madman searches for dreams
amongst midnight's stars,
shakes his fist
at the nightly constellations.
Onlookers crook their heads,
mouthing quiet prayers into the blood night air
-- secret whisperings of the silenced and the damned
-- legless, eyeless heroes,
rammed naked into boxcars (by Caesars' legions),
squeezing last, honest breaths out of one another's lungs.

They hang on to pass one spark,
one ember still glowing in the dark
-- from mouth to mouth, from eyeless eye to eyeless eye
-- fainted light for this night
imprinted deep in every newborn's awful cry,
hard within the stone of Promethean grief.

*

And they will say, 'He lived to trade heart for rock,
to start anew, so Virgin Brides need not despair;
desert blooms will catch the air.

And you will parrot back,
'There will come a day when Truth's flags will fly again!'

And a thousand ghosted, shrouded madmen
will intone,

> *'Never forget, never forget, never forget*
> *ohgodohgod... ohgodohgod... ohgodohgod....'*

The Belgian grays prick up their ears
and steal a silent prance.
A hot white sun beats down wet salt rays
upon all that would crawl beneath.

OBSIDIAN HEARTS

Men with obsidian hearts
came in the middle of the night.
They took her awake
to the isle of dread.

There, they bound her feet
and stole her thoughts.
They put her to sleep
and compelled others to forget.

There, the blacksmith forged
new horizons to shackle
onto old dreams
and to re-define reality.

Until it became
automatically so,
and the living
could not distinguish
from the dead.

But for the meadow-lark
that lived inside her
and sang its gentle tune.
They could not find it!
She, innocent, knew only

her beauty, not her power.
The seekers understood, though,
and lived in greater fear.

Each cold, dark night thereafter,
the meadow-lark sang.
At first plaintively, then hopefully,
eventually, with majesty.

Until it came to pass one day
the men with obsidian hearts
went away,
and children came out to play.

SOLITUDE

Disembodied hands
descend
the storm clouds --

Tiny dust refractors,
sparkling bits
of random light.

A blind man
taps a tune
on blue molten ice.

Breath levitates
like vapors
in the permafrost.

*

In the hollow
of our meadow
left still --

By absence
of any breeze --
we are within.

Ourselves,
alone but never abandoned.

Despair

Apparition II

One turns, these days,
in so many directions
through forgotten, revolving doors --
all shuttered by now.
She is, nevertheless,
everywhere:

In sun-tints bouncing off the glass,
rounded mirrors of passing eyes
always, in the end, striding
(I am convinced) toward me --
her embracing smile,
the movement of her hips,
the openness of her look.

'Come take me boldly --
but do it honestly and quickly, lest
we lose our way to the stars'.

The day of her birth is marked
upon rugged Celtic ground.
She stands, there,
head reared back,
proud thighs apart,
straddling mountaintops
breaching clouds, where
alpine streams flow.

She sings a soft refrain:
'loves won and lost
in another time'.

In my solitude
I reach out to receive
Her benediction.

ENIGMA

Eyes, into tunnels, merge
across the room.
No chatter, no interference
cull out the innocent.
No discourse, no distractions
enter the equation.

Lovers, darting, fleeing
-- they have no mouths --
like featureless animations
from a darker planet --
where innocence is for the taking,
where grace no longer suits.

Where dreams become sins entangled;
sins become skin for bones.

Vultures, on carrion-call
dive into the rot.

No kind words, no incantations
prevent the holocaust.
No distant stars, no crystal balls
light up this House of Carnage.

Children, abandoned, cease
their dragon slaying.
No suckled teat, no barbed wire
alter their fated course.

No Original Dream explodes the myth.
They slay each other.

Lovers -- even they(!) --
'soldier-sons of',
under-harried, fish smelling breath,
saluting golden gods --
marching lockstep to the tune of
'Ya-we, Ra-we, we'll do it our-way.'

No cosmic net, no self-trip-wires,
spring up to cushion this-kind's fall.

The soothsayer turns mute,
fool's bells on his cap.
Lovers, children, dreams, distant stars --
all that we are
-- tumble through a fog of tears,
the just and mad can no longer shed --

rivers of white-water tears,
ferrying us to forget
-- slow, gray oceans of tears,
lulling us through this dread sleep.

How is it, we can still weep (you ask)?
We weep -- Wagnerian tears, that's how.
Buckets-full for old loves
while we wring the necks of newly–born
-- fountains-full for dead dogs,
while we grab front row behind the glass.

How is it we can still witness (you ask)?
We keep the watch -- through ice veins, that's how.

We absorb in our skins
soft concertos, hard requiems. Still,
we stand dumb in the dock,
while the bride stains darkly, rusted-red.

*

Tunnels collapse into moats.
Moats into rivers, rivers into oceans.
No tears survive the final flood -
only salt!

The last men on earth mine the salt,
oblivious to the wild poppies
hugging, still, the reddened hillside
In the end, *nothing* matters – save the dead!

FOOTPRINTS IN THE SNOW

I searched for your footprints this winter.
I thought that I saw this last time --
faint remnants
where I wanted them to be:
tamped impressions,
where a moment's warmth had given way,
almost, to ice and anonymity.

Blinding snow sparkled there like mica crust
baking in the sun.
(Did we once hold each other,
so, in the glint of an eye?)
Cracked prisms -- these crystals
conjuring up a tapestry
of trompe l'oeils.

If I scoop a handful, they turn to melt.

Ancestor eyes are watching.
Their stones rise up snow capped
along my path.
Like a village of stationary ghosts,
they stand still-guard
o'er ancient longings left unsaid.

I become
quiet when I think of you.
Memories, here, are soft illusions
in the Gray; they *are alive.*
They dance
and curl like fire in hands that hold them.
If I close my fist, ever-more-so,
they turn to crystal.

Exquisite emptiness –
winter path.
A child would delight in its roundness.

For me, it bridles the real
in hoarfrost and desire --
and lets fly the essential
out her cold iron cage.

INNOCENCE PERISHED

You wear my heart
to touch an open wound.
Scraps of paste
feed a hungry beast.
No one may retaliate.
We can only endure.

A tall man drinks
robotically
in an empty space.
No lips to attach a smile.
No hands to hold a drink.
Osmosis lifts him up.

They call it spirit.
I call it death.
But it still beats:
thump-thump,
thump--thump.
I hold it in your throat.

Innocence perished here.
Crusts on iron filings,
brush calluses
on brave men's souls.
The damned ruled
in Hades one brief spell.

Here in darkness,
the nightingale
surrenders her voice,
swallows turn into bats,
young boys lose
their virginity.

Finger nails scrape
to defend against
imaginary ghouls;
eyes dart out of control.
The strong are
paralyzed.

In dank, painful fear,
human essence
is crushed
into a fine talc powder,
used to raise
disappearing ink.

A kind of sustainable
renewable...
this humankind.
Leaves God at the doorstep
and admires, from a distance,
her pruning.

Return to Dunskoi Graveyard

Children chat their ways –
birds on the edge of paradise,
running down hard packed snow paths
-- little legs carrying big eyes --
drawing nourishment (it seems)
from a bucket by the cemetery well.

Babushki, in impoverished grays,
trudge reverently down another,
spilling their precious priests' waste
down any number of ice holes.

Lovers stroll -- welded thigh to thigh,
embraced in soft, delicious
whisperings -- hot fantasies
for mingling winds and gaping souls.

Hundreds of stones stir like glaciers,
-- still, hooded, silent guardians,
holding down white crusted earth --
faded, dull flower stems in their teeth.

They cast late winter shadows --
dark, flat creatures -- weaving intricacies
on hallowed, beaten floor.
But they, too, are consumed by the snow.

A hundred stones, a thousand paths
center upon the well.
Too much white -- too much the perfect picture.
Thoughts obliterate, inner eyes submerge.
The well has no bottom.

Oblivion

A Howling Wind Runs Through Her[1]

She comes ferrying iron
through the stone age,
past monuments, heaped
      on sand -- rusted hieroglyphics
      clinging, all, to naught --
She, piercing myths, placing markers
o'er just men's graves.

Wide eyes, flickering on white ice
rising -- red-white petals floating,
on running waters –
she appears,
sweeping up ideas, religions
sophisms, like tumbleweed.

Casting dreams, roiling
through inlaid passageways,
past shipwreck timbers
left on nervous shores
of doubts heaped on steaming funeral pyres.

---

[1] After Graham Parker's song *Howlin' Wind*, in 1976 album *Howlin' Wind*.

Doubts and dreams that crash
into this fierce redoubt,
		hang on dying,
		whilst fresh recruits heed her call,
pulling up oars
to push against the currents.

Viking hair, a smile to swallow the moon,
long, straddle legs,
sweeping, plaintiff looks --
they wrap this she-wolf
that births our aspirations.

She comes finally to re-seed
		the petrified trees,
		left un-rooted,
waiting their winged avenger of
ten thousand snows ago.

She comes to clap her pale white hands
upon *my* heart,
a silver chalice, then,
or else, gated steel
		pounded into oblivion.

BETRAYAL OF A MAIDEN

Iron men came to take her away.
They hoisted her up
unto themselves
splayed
like a fatted calf
to be delivered to the spit.

Her life held no footnote.
She was, simply,
an *incidence*, duly recorded
on their most sensitive machines.

One note?
More like a riff, I think.
She was a *theme*, after all,
time capsuled
within the centerfold –
A beacon of sorts,
or better yet
a firefly that
lit up a
fragment of the way.

She held no false illusions.
Rather, she was
grateful for the moment.
Hers had been a wondrous Spring.

She was a goddess,
after all, to devour
like all true deities,
once the souls of iron men
came to gorge
upon themselves.

DARKENED HEART

Darkness comes to squat
o'er a still lake;
eyes may not yet penetrate.

One pale hand, pasted bloodless
on the canvas
reaches out
from the glassy wake.

'Mesdames, messieurs,
Faites vos jouets!'

A star chip, just then,
breaks off its canopy
lights up an old, wooden boat --

a single oar dipped
into the inky-black
vis-cos-ity.

One frail ribbon
of fragment's light
links the shadows,
cuts through the night.

Her whisper steals his breath --
    a garrote across his throat:

'The hour's late for dredging.
   I am the grail; I shan't be found.
Dark waters are my cove.'

A spider's lair
or strands of human hair?

Whatever!
The croupier extends his rake;
the chips tumble in.

 'Meine Damen und Herren,
machen ihre spiele!'

The only winner –
   he who has lost it all,
Grasps his luck with
   perfect, empty clarity.

Her hand, white on black,
becomes (for him) --
in a land of sunspots and dark erasures,
of hermit gods and
odd balanced scales --
center line for his masterpiece

(There - one may have his grail and eat it too.)

As for himself.

As for any pretender,
  the luckless widow
  bids him over…

Where Beelzebub's extractor
  remains in business
drawing current
  from proffered veins,

While a rope line of
human beings, across the way,
exhales in one wordless scream:
'We mourn for all un-captured truths!'

All the while -- I,
plunging ahead, naked
into the deep,
  to grasp for…

One Fine Day

There will come a winter day
when the attic trunk must open
(tarnished markers and all)
buried deep
with bits and pieces
of misplaced recollections --
salvation army dreams, all,
gravestones in my heart.

I suppose the hermit king or
wall street god may fear the same.
It would be said, within the space of time,
        we are all 'monks of the Order':
drunken priests, deceitful lovers,
pining widows squirreling
silver coins under mattresses
        -- the bloody common lot, you know.

But what of the garden?
There is that, too.
One need only hack through
the heavy vines and faded bougainvillea
to find traces
of original innocence.
Anemones and wild poppies
grew there, too.

Shouldn't that count as well?
Or is only the itemizing
of how many souls
piled high on the remains
-- like goggle-eyed tile fish
on the fisher's wharf --
to be counted in the reckoning?

Mind you, I have no fear of it,
this leafless, slate-gray day.
But I object to its arbitrariness!
I object to being lumped like coal
in with all the others,
counted and measured
like so many slaves
on the trading dock.

I would offer up my footprint --
my footprint!
After all, a man's oblivion
should be his own,
a quiet affair.

Shock Waves

Shock waves --
they roll over sharp iron filings
the way lions once ate Christians.

They roll over teeth, hair, combs, baby shoes,
invitations to a wedding,
the way hunger devoured Somalia.

They leave armored ants scurrying for cover,
dropping spoils, retracing circumlocutions,
the way the mad pace up and down talking to themselves.

They show no mercy,
penetrating between the plates which separate
the heart from other organs.

Pouring liquor down the throats of Muslims,
they ripple through the tear,
the way your cold eyes grab my breath.

To the Sea

A seer
once peered
into my cerebrum.

State-less,
she voyaged through its tropics
to bear this witness:
riptides,
alligator feasts, mad congresses
of imponderables.

Surgeon, white-robed,
steel scalpel in hand,
undoes magic knots
like so many bow-ties.

Holy man,
ragged,
penis in hand,
urinates on the wall
and casts no shadow.

A dark woman
in soft pastels
crosses the path,
one-hundred men
swivel their heads,
like jackals – in hot ejaculation.

Twelve Venetian masks
float above the kill,
sucking air through
opium reeds,
rooted in potting soil.

Specks of glitter –
fillips,
morsels,
in someone's giant crystal ball,
rented actors all.

TRAIN RIDE

He startles, awakened
-- synapses disconnected,
limbs wet in desert sweat,
salt water gagging lungs.
He is bled empty,
as if he has lost a child.

Images hold his eyes --
fuse like cellophane burning.
They smell of dead, raked leaves
and mulch into his heart,
-- black magic poultices
leached there by witches.

He forces back his head.
A long, slow, wretched scream
claws its way, gutturally --
solar plexus to throat,
-- to birth a gargoyle
through his stricken mouth.

*

The train has left the station.
The girl advances on him
--pale skin pricked by night frost,
brown nipples full erect,
red lipstick, soft lines.
He smiles a rueful smile
and turns to let her come.

He stands alone, naked,
arms strapped to trolley cross,
as if in supplication,
feet planted on wood slat floor,
-- on which to balance
Job's predicament,
through which, he counts -- the rails.

Around him, emptiness --
but for the odd assortment,
entrusted to Sherpas
in dark, mountain passes:
duffels, trunk, carrying bags,
safe deposit boxes -- stuffed full
with rubies, pearls and trinkets.

Center stage, by his side,
chained to one ankle,
like an old retainer --
a favorite, hide-bound case
-- a pride from early days
when dreams arrived in color,
shot from puffed wheat guns.

Design rules art in
this modern warrior's shield
-- its secrets less important
than polished sheen and
scent of old elephant --
butchered to create it.
Never leave home without it!

The train settles in its run.
The girl entangles one leg
about his waist and thigh
-- *in tango delicio.*
Her nipples still erect,
thin fingers on his neck,
she mounts and bites his ear.

Above his outstretched arms,
one naked, sooty bulb,
held over from a film noir,
spits out light to bleed away,
through crepe black windows
-- casting shadow here and there,
leaving dusk behind and near.

A faded time schedule,
flecked with dirty thumbprints,
peels -- posted by the door.
Faceless voices whisper
in requiem chorus.
His brain calculates the odds:
'Is this an opium den?'

Memories knock
on steel-cased barricades,
like shy brides
turned sea captains,
barking day's watch
-- cracked sheets of lightning,
blinding.

Solomon's treasures float
in rough sea around him.
(He'll never get them out.
How on god's earth have they gotten here?)
Just moments remain
to salvage one's lifetime!

The train is pulling in.
The girl shifts her balance,
unhinges the leg and
moves her hands upon his cock.
She begins to milk him slow,
like a bull, for semen,
meant to assuage the mares in heat.

Somewhere, a door slides open.
Bright, white light funnels in,
stage left, to illuminate
the penultimate aria --
a tapestry of
intermingled, rounded faces,
peers in with vague familiarity.

One arm frees to sweep grandly --
over his dominion.
'Here it is, here they are:
gemstones of my life.'
But eyes shifting through the scene
reflect chaos amongst his most precious things.
Picked clean, center stage,
the old elephant case --
skeleton bones on the plains.

Its underpinnings flapping --
unhinged, flayed -- soundlessly,
in absence of breeze.
Ice in his testicles.

Plunder -- liberation:
life's twin effigies.
Drowning, he pries, tugs, pummels
his hardscrabble booty --
to find that which he has lost
(but long ago commended
to seas sailed by Argonauts).

The train comes to rest.
The girl glides across him
in slower jerks and motions,
like amperage winding down
the film projector --
lips smacking,
whistling *gottsegnederfuehrer*
through her teeth.

They grind on, clickety clack,
clickety clack, c l i c k e t y c l a c k

-- while the movie runs on --
to full stop.
He, enigma, becomes a frieze,
painted into hollowed shells of trains.
She becomes powder for the paint.

Booty turns to rags:
kerchiefs for babushki,
pennants for tips
of crusader lances,
parchment for Abyssinians,
masks to shield from cholera.
Dust to dust....

*

It -- has No departure.
There -- is No time.
We -- make No choices.
I -- have No exit.

He forces back his head --
the farthest back it will go.
A puff of smoke wafts
through the scream --
the slightest smile,
curled around distended lips.
The conductor takes his ticket.

Yesterday's Child

He lived among us in splendid isolation
with glorious glass house views

      *

Alone at the altar,
the surprised bridegroom
who has forgotten his ring
--he stares, beyond the would-be veil, to see
black-ink swirls greeting black-ink swirls.

Cloud dust rains upon yesterday's child
-- soft, protective smother on ragged, ancient cheeks.
Hushed, abandoned lyrics trickle down
-- chewing up and eating wormholes
in a buried place
long forgotten for its memories:

Tiny, distant moments --
Easily unassuming, they mimic
miniature blinking Christmas lights,
bubbling over
into some dark, unwashed corner.

His, a life never bartered, only bargained
-- given, un-chosen, to predators and the winds,
made un-attended, left enigmatic,
like a garden gone to seed.

He tries to gulp down anything he can find,
to restore a living, breathing self.
But he tilts, instead, at phantoms.
In the end,
memories are enigmas, too.

A midnight fugue echoes in his bones
hauling up so many, plaintiff arias --
flopping, still, helter-skelter,
for an air no longer breathed.

*

Nothing live accompanies him,
this yesterday's child.
No texture clings.
Colorless and odorless mist suffice for sky;
color, for any sake is ablated.
Nuance has fled for the hills;
no warming fire blazes in the stove.

His, a destiny imprisoned by hubris
-- shuttered up inside
bulletproof sheets of glass,
indifferent to drifting snows
or miracles of any kind.

Ever the conjurer,
he tries to dream up
first the innocent,
then the damned.

So long as he remains ambivalent,
it matters not against whom and for what
reasoning -- he chooses to duel.
Only, he has misplaced the point of it!

An emptiness settles in
like ice packed, burned flesh
-- or suspended animation,
the frozen dead long to have.

He peers out at us with sightless eyes,
bearing witness to everything and nothing.
We shout back and forth words of encouragement —
He is one of us! One of us! But we can
no more leapfrog the sun than save his soul.

*

We spectators line up,
witnesses to the execution
-- with church belfries and organ baffles
pasted on chalk-white countenances
-- giving echo to a hollow wind.
Nearby, shadows beckon us all
and we know not who, when or why
the next must go.

Wonder

A Place by the Sea

There is a place
by the sea
where lovers' secrets hide.

Wild poppies bloom
in shipwrecked sands,
lip rouged in midnight sun.

Ice blue sheets
of winter glass
reflecting shuttered thoughts.

Lay cover
to the hidden mound
of the underbelly.

Polished black volcanic rock
compels a mountain stillness.

Like fat sea lions
lulled to sleep
on alpine moss.

Luminescent vapors
embrace the contours.

Seamlessly,
shamelessly,
they shake one's hold.

I drift here
in surrender
to your caressing eyes.

BIRCHES

The birches standing on the bank
indulge the snow to settle
in their shade,

As the moon, hanging on a thread
obliges lovers to couple
in its glow.

Your tears fall upon my heart
like drops of stinging rain,
boring holes

Deep into the forest
where the snow leopard hides
among the birches.

EDGE TIDES

Wavelets...
shimmer
surface light
-- like hungry minions
impatient,
garrulous,
ever advancing.
Platoon like,
they sweep their
remorseless, silvery arch.

Bright smiles...
pillars of light,
like so many flash bulbs.
Stieglitz --
capturing her shadows:
undulating
peaks and valleys,
in black and white.
Glimpses of secrets
in the folds.

Beneath...
within the sanctum,
no flags for independence fly.

A switch is thrown;
clockwork shifts to high,
or to glide,
or to frieze,
upon the still --
until the entire corpus
mimics sheet glass.

Above...
under God's eye,
a dervish
strokes his beard
and calls upon the wind.
Tides begin to drift --
subtle vapors:
some whirl into sinkholes
like toy trains
going 'round the mountain.

ESSENCE

Silent impressions
penetrate the nonsense
yet will no one
rescue portent?

Useless, small things
jar loose
delicious thoughts:

Soft petals
in red wine goblets,
lip rouged and curled

Streamers
in a young girl's
long braided hair

Easter eggs
hollowed out,
sucked dry for the hunt

Colored glass
pasted bits in
a child's mosaic

Crystal
dreams hanging on to
spider threads

Stuff of whims
lion tamers, fakirs
fashion our trance

Silken wombs
entomb
our joy

In the Basement of the British Museum

An Atlas heart within --
waiting patiently, through all of winter's outing --
cried out to no one in particular,
time is fiction, perfection eternal,
Old friend.

*

I found him in a forgotten corner,
This blond beast of Halicarnassus
Amidst the bits and pieces
Strewn together
-- Abandoned through the ages
To a distant mausoleum
Beneath the Piccadilly line.

A hundred years of dust
Sparkled on his alabaster mane,
But I knew him straight away.
His eyes drank in the reflection – smiling through,
They dwell.

As if to say,
'We have been waiting,
Waiting for you, old friend,
To drift to us again.

We have seen much since the Superstition.
Tombs are emptied, specters scattered,
But our heart beats on.'

And with that,
Like the nomad who finds his spring
I placed my eyes upon the snow
And touched my lips to the stone,
As if to say, "You are all that I have known."

Warm flesh /cold rock.
I embraced this gentle guardian of the tomb,
Seventh Wonder from an ancient womb,
-- Threw my arms in thief's abandon
'Round his marble mane –
Absolved myself of mystery.

*

And when, at last, all the ghosts inside
Awoke to mount their beasts.
It did not matter!
Nothing mattered, save the tears,
Big, grateful, moonstones
Come to tumble down the
Cheeks of Ararat.

'How are you, old friend?
So many instants,
So few recognitions.
We have come a long way

To find ourselves again.'
(Hard comfort, still,
From those chiseled truths
Carried o'er his body
-- Like so many tattoos
Or iron staked crucifixes!)

'I kiss your mane, timeless heart
And carry your spirit to my grave.'

For a moment, there,
I turned –
Good soldier
And the needy lover,
Then, to clay
That last wintry day.

Precepts dissolved
Into ancient sculpted images,
Painted over with desert varnish
To confuse the senses and hide
The holy passages.

Perhaps, I was tired or lonely.
For a brief interruption
I was nothing and my heart was full.
Perhaps, my imagination was hungry.
Or maybe, just maybe… I was.

GHOSTS

You see, my love,
the portals close, eventually.
They fold in upon themselves,
like petals,
ever so shyly,
to leave us sightless.

Perhaps, only ghosts may see
the desert orchids prepare
their sunset.

We neglect the smallest things:
take portraits in lockets.

In Gargantuan

On the mighty arc of the great Roc
she sits, carelessly --
a pale white leg dangling,
one bare arm draped lightly,
over the monster's neck.
Long, slender, red flicked fingers
tickling the hoary mane.

A tiny, mauve-pink *jupe*
tucked loosely 'round her waist.
A fiery, come-hither smile –

They are my pas de deux,
in gargantuan,
sculpted from amber block,
splashed by sun
rooted in potting soil.

A bouquet from Roerich's palette,
a grand erection for Miller's Tropics.
She haunts my shadows.

Seventeen

I remember
In a mist
Long legs
No stockings
Summer heat
Spiked heels
On cobble stone
Thick musk air
Girls in slow motion
Henry Miller's Tropics
10 francs a copy
Red lettered tattoos
Sailors on leave
Men cruising
St. Denis
Sweet hyacinth
In the air
The river Seine
The curve
of her naked backside.

SHA-LA-NA-NA-NA

The master spider's handiwork
plays no favorites.
It spins justice
    only in our dreams.

Contradicting thoughts course
through narrow cobbled passageways.
They weave mazelike
    and disguise the moon.

Hard packed earth echoes back
refrains locked in crystal hearts.
It presses in
    upon thoughts still living.

At moments like this
I take your cool smile into mine.

And the music-man sings
    sha-la-na-na-na...

My Father's Watch

I

In a secret place
I kept a plain, tin box,
with a well-traveled look
-- a musketeer's field kit,
perhaps, upon its time.

A master had
etched there, in large red markings,
on her dull, metal base,
vague, dusky landscapes
-- no doubt, to blunt the glitter
of Monte Cristo's cellar:
one hollow bar of gold,
come wrapped in
fine, Easter tinsel
present paper,
until banquet night.

When sparkling, multicolored gemstones
could come tumbling out
and be caressed
in the itchy palms of a
small boy's hidden appetites.

Innocent beginnings,
these were my most precious things

II

A thick wad
of doubly folded
Stolypin paper,
crisp to the touch,
smelling fresh from the mint.

Brought out
one moonless night
from Petersburg,
by Grandfather Sasha,
near the time when Vladimir Ilyich died.

An emerald stickpin,
platinum set --
worn by Great Aunt Helen
across one proud,
upward tilting breast
on her Cotillion day.

Two alabaster pipes --
one, cherry red,
the other, teeth marks
in the stem,
a ram's head for the fill.

Carved and smoked
by my mother's father,
in old Antwerp,
while apprenticed to Jews
cutting diamonds by his side.

A fist-sized rock
streaked with veins of gold,
silver, lead and quartz --
its full, dead weight:
a fist-full of shot from Olympiad.

Pick-axed on a climb
with Uncle Logi de B.,
on Chapultepec's
highest granite cliffs,
in thin, cleansing air.

Three racing marbles,
baked brown-red in the
mud tubs of St. Miguel
-- won (by me) the year
Saint Nicholas went away.

And – wrapped
in soft, velvet housing
(still, in its maker's
Tiffany case, reserved, once, for
the finest of offerings to
princes, dukes and what-nots) --
My father's watch!
It was the most beautiful
watch for telling time, its mechanism
the most rational in creation --
given to me when it was time.

White-gold-rimmed,
in perfect winding order,
soft green phosphorescent letters,
black alligator strapped, she was first
revealed, thus, to me.

III

Just *the idea of it* --
much subtler than reality!
On *my* wrist, its second hand
could sweep beyond eternity,
to touch across the stars.

It would be as if I
could read Akhmatova
in her own hand. I could
raise each letter, each word,
each stanza -- to the sky and
feel, alongside, her inmost passion.
I could be there!

IV

A man
dances his jig
around his goods,
a boy in search of his journey,
around his dreams.

Prizes,
locked in
hidden sanctity,
shaped my dreams.

I treasured them
and hoarded
their significance,
while, all the while,
searching --
for the perfect metaphor.

And wondering,
wandering,
about circles
within circumferences,
proscribed around my time.

Fog light skimming
on sea foam,
floating memories
in a private crystal ball,
drifting grains of sand from Atlantis.

V

I dreamt, then, in vivid colors --
expressionist, futurist, Dadaist, Warholian
colors -- pressed
against my entire being.
So hopeful --

In my dreams
I would fly, often, to other places,
steering casually,
with head and heart,
keeping ballast in the spine.

Like Spartacus, I thought,
giving himself
over to death
in airborne abandon.
(Yet never lacking grace!)

I traveled where I dreamed,
or where, perhaps
it was dreamed for me.
(Is that all we are about:
embryonic two-steps
in someone else's choreography?)

VI

Seedlings draped in longings
have a way
of blending into
more precious things --
they birth early callings.

Will, imagination --
the wind,
stir the wanderlust;
Its grubby root
(I think, today) is hubris.

The wanderer
drags his tattered body
across the precipice,
around the bend --
to grasp for -- the pinnacle.

The pinnacle
of what, you ask --
the peak of the Himalayas?
Apex of uncovered ruins?
Or the mount between
the virgin bride's clutching thighs?

The old prospector
rolls out from
his hermit cabin,
morning smoke
in perpetual stasis.

Pick and shovel
strapped to back
-- vacant, pre-determined
look upon his mug --
to play *out* the ritual.

A ritual?
For what, you ask --
fame or filthy riches -- alone?
Or to be the bigger fool
to one's coveted gold?

The old prospector resembles
the ancient sea tortoise,
returning, one upon the other,
again, again -- to bury its eggs
in sterile sand.

VII

Sooner or later
The second hand stops
Dreams dry up,
prayer descends --
in a last defense to protect the quest.
'Father, I chose you.

I wear your watch
to encircle time --
and navigate around poets,
prospectors, wanderers
and ancient sea tortoises.

May I know, now (!)
what it is you have
in store for me?
Is there a place
whose air I may gulp down whole?
Whose scent shall be
my primal smell?
Whose visibility shall fit
my own sense of three dimensionality?
Whose ground will envelop
my footprint?

Whose embrace
will blanket my pain?'

The cameraman smiles
his holographic smile!
We step parade our longings
like tin soldiers guarding
the palace.

VIII

Memories of my tin box
and the things inside
long ago receded
into mythology.
Prayers for saving grace
feasted on themselves --
soundless thunderclaps
in forgotten cloudbursts,
whose tears washed
out to sea.

Lucky souls in the drift
fall onto Ishmael's path.
Before they are gone,
they are returned -- old men
with faded penis sheathes --
content for once
with what must be,
satisfied to sift through gems
with blind, un-seeking eyes
that glitter deep inside.

But the search
for buried treasure
is the Golden Fleece!
I wear the watch
these remaining hours,
like Jason's bracelet --
to mark the richness
of my time,
and to steer around
imagined truths.

Fools and gorgons
may still rush to war
in search of fathers, too.
Demagogues
may still thrive on
a million souls a day,
and march them
to their end to simplify – and to
stake their claim
on their reality.

In the end, though,
answers are buried like
eggs in the sand.
They do not matter.
Imponderables propel the dance.
Innocence remains a lonely mystery.

THE WHITE

I *Redemption*

The old dust woman bows deeply
as the carriage passes
-- its big wooden wheels spinning
soft circles in winter's first snow.

Two black mounts
gallop in the lead, snorting
white mist into a Merlin sky
-- 'God's breath' to the old woman's eye.

In the passing vision,
faces to the wind, two lovers
hold so close -- as if to let go their grip
would be to lose the other
over the steepest cliff.

Tall firs stand guard their route.
A winter hare dashes for its life.
A white moon skates on crystal
and races frost shadows -- skimming.

II *Retribution*

In another world across the sea,
the hour marks a flick
beyond the 0 --
all space lies collapsed
upon Everyman's horizons --

Through which,
an endless caravan of just glazed figures
moves as in a daze through
the opposites of night and day --
one leg up, one leg down -- trudging
dustless, mirrored dunes
under hot white sun --

Glassy souls on the march,
awaiting, forward staring,
moving naked -- into the White,
like scales of the snake
coiled around an absent universe.

In the tiny hollow remaining,
an old beggar holds out
his beggar's bowl
and draws forth the rain
to bless the caravan.

III *Release*

Their escape is accidental
-- a momentary distortion in the
almsman's field of vision,
he mistakes them for
an inconsequential flight of candlelight
down a quiet country river.

Raindrops, perfect in their isotropic state,
falling… nowhere, refracting rainbows
in the circle of their sun --
fall upon the White and begin to freeze,

as if in terror of the next,
until virgin snow, in its wedding dress,
drifts down and begins to melt --

Until two fragile beings, then, chancing to be conceived,
are freed, sent spinning -- in aimless, broken symmetry.

IV *Renewal*

Caught between fragments of different worlds,
they race on, suspended
through threads of fairy tales
in the cold, night air.

Their carriage, a bauble
in a giant's hand,
like a child's crystal ball
to be shaken in delight --

In which lovers float like silent stars
and dare not breathe --
lest the moon change its orbit
and snow turn to glass.

In the quiet rush
a faint whistle of wind
slices across their hearts.
A secret, primeval whisper
nibbles out from within.

Acknowledgements

I am a first-time published author of a poetry book. As such, at one level, I owe thanks to the world for putting up with my boyish enthusiasm and constantly encouraging me to forgo my natural intimidation when confronted by so many good poets just waiting to be read. There is, of course, another level. This is one of even (I believe) excessive support of my passion to write and publish a book of poetry. My early readers come to mind, led by the likes of Michael Schaffer, Natalya Romanova, Ulf Runquist and David Deaver Brown.

There are a few special later readers, who had some particular contributions to make and whom I want to thank for their persistence in staying the course with a manuscript that turned out to be a longer read than promised. David Field, Naomi Foner, Jane Marlo Robbins – stand up, please and take a bow!

Two wonderful women inspired me during the early days. Margo Viscusi was a picture of quiet confidence when it came to any discussions of me taking up the mantle of a poet – a *real* poet. She is a lifelong President Emerita of Poets House. At Margo's urging, Phillis Levin became for a brief moment my teacher, chief critic and agitator. And in the course of a handful of weekly sessions she became effectively my first editor. A Fulbright Scholar with multiple degrees, Phillis is also the author of several books of poetry, including *Temples and Fields*, *Mercury*, and *Mr. Memory & Other Poems*.

More recently, there are those who helped to shape the final product, who need to be acknowledged: Andreas Coronas, who has served as line editor, and Michael Hardy, who has recently joined the team as principal narrator to complete the reader's choice of having in his or her hands a real live book with paper pages and artwork, or an audiobook with all the benefits that provides.

And, then, there is Fran Forman – an exciting surrealist artist who has designed all of the cover art and chapter illustrations for this book. Fran travels the world offering up seminars, "best" in-kind photography exhibits and one-woman shows; her work is included in major museums and private collections. There is quiet darkness that attaches to her work that almost gives way to revelation as she strides to integrate her art with photography and, now, in this project with poetry as well. Thank you, Fran!

Finally, there is a surprise that I very much want to share with the reader. I want to share the secret sauce – the secret inspiration – that has kept me going throughout these more recent, more difficult times as we moved nearer to the closure of this project and to the inevitable stripping away of any remaining protective garb aimed at hiding the true level of all my inadequacies.

And so, we come to a young man who came into my life just sixteen years ago. He is my grandson and he has written a poem. But not just a poem. A great poem. One to ponder on. One that won Arion Carraher-Kang national recognition among tens of thousands of competing young writers and poets. This poem together with Arion's gentle but firm manner of delivery won my heart and has given me all that I needed to muster my own courage. So, thank you Arion and here is your poem:

Latino Story:
Voices of Immigrants

Beginning.
When, at first, all was dark, beneath the skies of Oaxaca
Only the glow of the kitchen could reach me.
Mamá, in her bright huipil soaked the pork and hummed to son
istmeño, Her motions caught in the sugar speckled light as she
worked.
Mamá, who scolded me for clumsily coating myself in flour.
Mamá, who told me,
told me I was her little angel.
That "No one can ever take that away from you."
She kissed me on the temple
And sent me to
My papá, who whispered to me,
mi niño, my child,
Do you see there, the stars how they shine in your name?
I stared past his finger into the night.
Where papá?
He laughed.
"Of course, Francisco, you are one who is free
A star above the world.
You don't need to see to know it's there."

el estío
The morning struck violently in the summer,
Bleeding orange on the horizon, the rind broken from the sun
turning sticky,
peeling back the pooling shade
as it rose above lazy clouds.
My sister Amalure and I would play,
Running through Mercado Benito Juárez

Our bare feet tapping the ground as the stones seared our skin.
Only in the house or beneath the Árbol del Tule was there an
escape, The coolness sinking into us as we panted.
There we would sit,
Picking at the coiled Corredor Mexicano.

We knew it could not hurt us.
Only hiss and writhe in the dirt as it escaped into the blaze.

comida para el alma
Every week
on our way through the market,
I would clutch Mama's list, damp in my dusty hands, as my sister
pulled at my arms
hoping to see the rushed, half slanted instructions.

*2 sacos de masa, 1 pollo del simpático carnicero. 1 bolsa de plátano deja un
poco de mantequilla*

My sister and I would work quickly,
awaiting the warmth of the kitchen that seeped into us.
Drenching us in the spirit of the Mole that had been simmering for
hours.
We would stare in wonder as Mamá reached about,
Throwing Everything into the pot
The chiles, the spices, the sweet fruits, the sour tomatillos, the nuts
which helped thicken the sauce.
At the end, Mamá would add the chocolate.
Turning the muck a wonderful deep shade of brown,
Like the earth, softened by rain.
Its scent wafting through the building, sticking to the walls,
and out into the darkening skies.

bajo las estrellas

Beneath the stars, mijo, you are beneath your stars. See how they shine in your name.

But papá, we have come so far. So far from home.
Whose stars are these? Where is Mamá? Where is Amalure?

Hush now we are close, very close. Soon we will be home. Soon we will be free.

But then I was still, un niño tonto, a silly little boy.
I could not take to heart the meaning of freedom, I had always *been* free.
I prayed silently and clutched papá's hand as he led me through the night.

I called to my stars one last time.

trabajo
The industrial light flickered,
Casting dim,
lazy tendrils of light
That sat and vanished from the peeling plaster eggshell walls of the restaurant. Here, there was no comfort of my memories.
I never felt the warm glow of the kitchen,
never saw
Mamá's pursed lips as she danced.
Never felt the food embrace me.
Not again.
I felt spiritless as I worked.

Solo
I guess I am like my father.
We share our hair, our eyes, our memories, and our dreams. We had melded together.

So,
as I sat alone,
Older now, but not old enough.
I realized,
Mamma was wrong.
All these years being free had stripped me.
Now my silhouette filled a foggy mirror, No halo, no smile.

Barely like an angel.

AFTERWORD

I am at heart a storyteller, and my poetry is largely narrative. I am grateful to those early readers who have found stylistic similarities between my work and the likes of such giants as Chekhov, Milosz, Keats and Stevens. That is high praise, and I am sage enough to take these compliments for what they are worth: fleeting moments of exuberance. This does not mean that I am not ambitious, as I long for the reader who will re-read my poetry to pause and think deeply. Above all, give me a reader who surrenders, when reading my poetry, thought to feeling in pursuit of a highly personal, emotive experience.

Some of my poems are only a handful of lines, such as *I Open* and *Birches*. Others, like *Tryptic in 3D* and *Histories I-II*, are combinations of poems meant to be read all at once if not in quick succession of each other. My ultimate goal is for the reader to be inspired by their favorite lines and poems – much like the fictional hero from *Max Skylight of the Skylight Chronicles* (another writing of mine).

About the Poet and His Poetry: Why a "Russian Collection?"

These forty-seven poems constitute the core of a body of work mostly written during an intensive period of my life, which circled around my last two years in Russia (1996-'98) and my first three years back in the U.S.A (1999 – '02) – but not personally compiled nor edited until fifteen years later (2015 – '19), by a different man – one who had been blessed, who had escaped, endured, witnessed, loved and been loved, profoundly changed.

Russia looms large in my poetry, if only as the central metaphor. So does a continuing search for self over, figuratively, three "lifetimes".

I went to Russia for several reasons: to find and claim my roots; to help the New Russians where I could; to witness the fall of a totalitarian empire, which, save for the Nazi terror, proved to be more corrupt and deep-rooted than any that had come before in our most murderous and unreasoning twentieth century. Life advanced predictably. I rented an apartment outside the sector typically reserved for *иностранец* (*inostranets - foreigners*), formed an all-Russian merchant bank to invest in the new Russian economy, began to collect art, reverted back to smoking, started reading and writing poetry, even developed a taste for Russian *standard* vodka, all the while, retreating more and more to the arias in my Sony Walkman. I was becoming...

Every day in Russia was an adventure. One day, early on, I was reluctantly shaking the hand of the newly installed Acting-President of the Soviet Union. I cannot, to this moment, get out of my mind how much longer than mine his hand kept shaking.

Later that fall ('91), I found myself debating in my small apartment - the, then, chief economic advisor to President Yeltsin. What a stunning display of the weaponization of hypocrisy -- Boris Yeltsin, man of peace, who will be forever revered for having stood astride the top of a brand-new Soviet tank '91 issue and single-handedly turned back a Revolution, interdicted a coup, and pointed communist Russia in a completely new direction.

The subject was the ruble and relative State asset values. The economic advisor, after a lot of "soul searching", opted to revise the ruble value downward from its current 1:1 tie to the dollar. Continue to fix the ruble to the dollar and peg it down to around 1:1.6; "but be prepared to pay the consequences". I was equally cryptic: bankrupt the ruble, privatize industry, I argued. For several years we would never know how close the "bankruptcy option" was to providing a real solution.

But, then, there would have been oligarchs, culture and corruption to consider – none of which were even on the table at the time. If only we had known! Solutions on paper, or around a coffee table loaded up with sweets for my guest's rumored sweet tooth, came relatively early-on -- the implementation of these seemed to take forever.

Almost two years later (October, '93) a "Constitutional" crisis arrived in Moscow with what was reported to be the fiercest street fighting in Moscow ever since the October Revolution of 1917. Then President Yeltsin ordered up an elite tanks corps and camouflaged, armored personnel carriers to oust rebel lawmakers and their families from the national Parliament (the Russian White House) after eleven days and nights of siege. Reportedly, hundreds were wounded and killed in this assault and coordinated attack on unarmed protesters at Ostankino -- the principle Moscow based television broadcasting tower.

Across the river, mingling with press and other "dignitaries", well in advance of military lines, we watched behind yellow military tape, while 20-30 elite corps tanks lobbed shells through the open windows of the Russian White House, trying not to kill any more renegade lawmakers and their families hiding out, in the white marble building -- nor to incur any added costs in anticipation of contracted Turkish renovations.

Then, there were the three *Hare Krishnas* in full hair regalia, in a connecting tunnel with near perfect acoustics, shaking their music makers while swaying to the beat; or who could ever forget the pretty girl stepping out onto the running board of one of these tanks, adjusting the standard issue side view mirror with one hand while reaching for a lipstick tube with the other?

For that matter, I will never forget dropping in on future Governor Zhenia Nazdratienko's massive strip-mining operations, in an army tin can helicopter just waiting for inclement weather or an accident-prone pilot. I remember when future Russian Prime Minister Tolia Chubais, gathered up City Deputies in St. Petersburg to exhort the then, *City Committee on Foreign Affairs* to burn their Communist membership cards.

A day, then, in Russia was a day of extraordinarily big, generous hopes and dreams, coupled in irony with a clear, Gogol-like sense of the ridiculousness of it all. What of the big city mayor who kept a collection of Lenin Heads in the basement – waiting for the first Western flim-flam artist to come along to help sell them? The deal went nowhere, but it remained barely alive – if not comatose – since in Russia there is no such thing as a *dead deal.*

Or what about a head-to-toes *(ochin priatna)* greeting lineup of leaders of a formerly "closed" city producing outer space delivery systems exclusively for the State -- from the first leader with a hundred-million-dollar plan to renovate the complex to the eighth in line, who proposed a one-million-dollar investment in a brick factory to support local housing production.

There is a story, here, of course – and it is not just about some starry-eyed American, trying to find himself in middle age. Nor is it the political science scoop of the century -- that profound and lasting political/economic change comes only with cultural change and *that* requires *several* generations to bring about. I put my poetry down sometime in 2003, forgot entirely about this collection for the balance of the decade, before subjecting the entire work to a daunting, personal edit over the past couple of years. I know it is a "rough" and highly personal collection. Excellence, I believe, hides somewhere under the fold; the story, like a good bottle of red, improves with age.

Alex Levitch has crafted a forty year career founding and launching early stage ventures as well as structuring and negotiating a wide variety of complex partnerships and acquisitions ranging from mass distributed baby products to acquisition of a major airline to on-line teacher professional development to an integrated Moscow based Russian investment house.

He holds a B.A. in Political Science from the University of Michigan and a J.D. *cum laude* from Columbia Law School and is a former assistant prosecutor for the U.S. Department of Justice.

Together with his wife, Linda, he lives and writes on the northern shore of Lake George in upstate New York on the edge of a fabled, hundred-year-old children's summer camp -- Adirondack Camp *adirondackcamp.com*, which Alex and Linda acquired almost forty years ago and resuscitated around a campaign entitled "Camp was so much fun I bought it!"